Tomie dePaola

Mice Squeak, We Speak

A Poem by Arnold L. Shapiro

SCHOLASTIC INC.

New York Toronto London Auckland Sydney
Mexico City New Delhi Hong Kong

Cats purr.

roar·roar·roar·

Lions roar.

Owls hoot.

Bears snore.

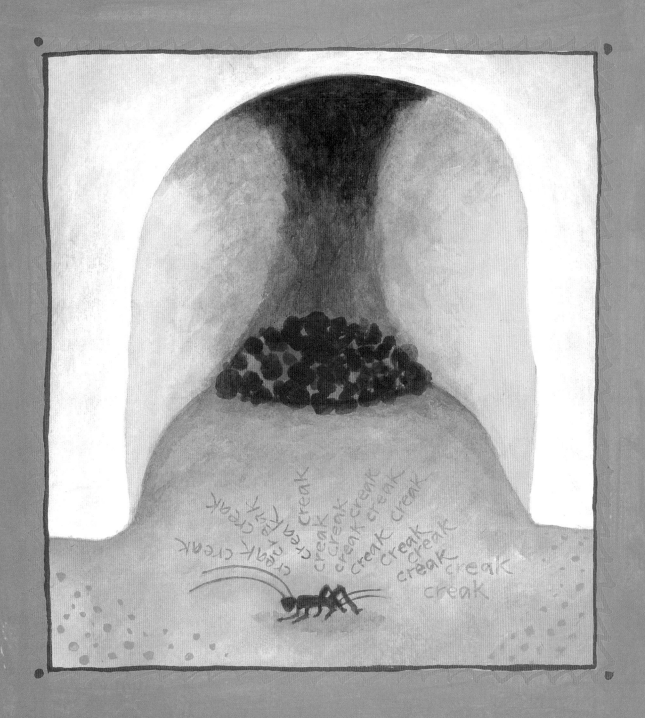

Crickets creak.

Mice squeak.

Sheep baa.

Monkeys chatter.

Cows moo.

Ducks quack.

Doves coo.

Pigs squeal.

neigh.

Horses neigh.

Chickens cluck.

Flies hum.

Dogs growl.

Bats screech.

Coyotes howl.

Frogs croak.

Parrots squawk.

Bees buzz.

For Fraser Anthony

my Aussie godson

and his Mama and Papa, Jenny and Tony

ISBN 0-590-38666-2

Text copyright © 1984 by World Book, Inc.
Illustrations copyright © 1997 by Tomie dePaola.
Original title "I Speak, I Say, I Talk."
All rights reserved.
Published by Scholastic Inc., 555 Broadway, New York, NY 10012,
by arrangement with G.P. Putnam's Sons, a division of the
Putnam & Grosset Group.
SCHOLASTIC and associated logos are trademarks and/or registered
trademarks of Scholastic Inc.

12 11 10 9 8 7 6 5 4 3 2 1   9/9 0 1 2 3 4/0

Printed in the U.S.A.   08

First Scholastic printing, January 1999